BUSY, BUSY LEAVES

By NADIA HIGGINS
Illustrations by CHRIS BIGGIN
Music by DREW TEMPERANTE

CANTATA LEARNING

WWW.CANTATALEARNING.COM

CANTATA
LEARNING

Published by Cantata Learning
1710 Roe Crest Drive
North Mankato, MN 56003
www.cantatalearning.com

A note to educators and librarians from the publisher: Cantata Learning has provided the following data to assist in book processing and suggested use of Cantata Learning product.

Publisher's Cataloging-in-Publication Data
Prepared by Librarian Consultant: Ann-Marie Begnaud
Library of Congress Control Number: 2016938071
Busy, Busy Leaves
Series: My First Science Songs
By Nadia Higgins
Illustrations by Chris Biggin
Music by Drew Temperante
Summary: Learn how leaves help plants make food through photosynthesis in this illustrated story set to music.
ISBN: 978-1-63290-785-1 (library binding/CD)
ISBN: 978-1-68410-108-5 (paperback)
Suggested Dewey and Subject Headings:
Dewey: E 575.57
LCSH Subject Headings: Photosynthesis – Juvenile literature. | Leaves – Juvenile literature. | Photosynthesis – Songs and music – Texts. | Leaves – Songs and music – Texts. | Photosynthesis – Juvenile sound recordings. | Leaves – Juvenile sound recordings.
Sears Subject Headings: Photosynthesis. | Leaves. | School songbooks. | Children's songs. | Popular music.
BISAC Subject Headings: JUVENILE NONFICTION / Science & Nature / Botany. | JUVENILE NONFICTION / Music / Songbooks. | JUVENILE NONFICTION / Science & Nature / Flowers & Plants.

Book design and art direction: Tim Palin Creative
Editorial direction: Flat Sole Studio
Music direction: Elizabeth Draper
Music written and produced by Drew Temperante

Printed in the United States of America in North Mankato, Minnesota.
072017 0367CGF17

TIPS TO SUPPORT LITERACY AT HOME

WHY READING AND SINGING WITH YOUR CHILD IS SO IMPORTANT

Daily reading with your child leads to increased academic achievement. Music and songs, specifically rhyming songs, are a fun and easy way to build early literacy and language development. Music skills correlate significantly with both phonological awareness and reading development. Singing helps build vocabulary and speech development. And reading and appreciating music together is a wonderful way to strengthen your relationship.

READ AND SING EVERY DAY!

TIPS FOR USING CANTATA LEARNING BOOKS AND SONGS DURING YOUR DAILY STORY TIME

1. As you sing and read, point out the different words on the page that rhyme. Suggest other words that rhyme.
2. Memorize simple rhymes such as Itsy Bitsy Spider and sing them together. This encourages comprehension skills and early literacy skills.
3. Use the questions in the back of each book to guide your singing and storytelling.
4. Read the included sheet music with your child while you listen to the song. How do the music notes correlate to the words of the song?
5. Sing along on the go and at home. Access music by scanning the QR code on each Cantata book. You can also stream or download the music for free to your computer, smartphone, or mobile device.

Devoting time to daily reading shows that you are available for your child. Together, you are building language, literacy, and listening skills.

Have fun reading and singing!

When we are outside, leaves are all around us. Trees, bushes, and flowers have leaves. Even blades of grass are leaves. Whenever the sun is out, leaves are working. They use sunlight to make food out of air and water.

To learn more about busy, busy leaves, turn the page and sing along!

One, two, three, four, five, six!
Six plant parts and they go like this:
roots, stems, leaves,
flowers, fruit, and seeds!

Each part plays a special role.
Leaves help plants to grow and grow.

Leaves do not hunt. They do not chew.
Busy leaves make plant food.
From sunlight, air, and water,
leaves help plants make food.

Busy, busy, busy leaves
doing things we cannot see.
When busy leaves make food, it's not a trick.
It's called **photosynthesis**! Photosynthesis!

Come on over into the shade,
where leaves flutter, bend, and sway
on roses, grasses, and pine trees.

Broad, thin, or **spiky**—they're all leaves!

Leaves do not hunt. They do not chew.
Busy leaves make plant food.
From sunlight, air, and water,
leaves help plants make food.

Busy, busy, busy leaves
doing things we cannot see.
When busy leaves make food, it's not a trick.
It's called photosynthesis! Photosynthesis!

Farmers grow leaves that are good for you.
Leaves are food that you eat, too:
lettuce, spinach, and **kale** galore,
cabbage, **collards**, and so much more!

Be a tree with your leaves up high.
Reach toward the sun and sway side to side.
Plant your feet like they're tree roots.
Be a tree making yummy plant food.

Leaves do not hunt. They do not chew.
Busy leaves make plant food.
From sunlight, air, and water,
leaves help plants make food.

Busy, busy, busy leaves
doing things we cannot see.
When busy leaves make food, it's not a trick.
It's called photosynthesis! Photosynthesis!

Leaves do not hunt. They do not chew.
Busy leaves make plant food.
From sunlight, air, and water,
leaves help plants make food.

Busy, busy, busy leaves
doing things we cannot see.
When busy leaves make food, it's not a trick.
It's called photosynthesis! Photosynthesis!

SONG LYRICS

Busy, Busy Leaves

One, two, three, four, five, six!
Six plant parts and they go like this:
roots, stems, leaves,
flowers, fruit, and seeds!

Each part plays a special role.
Leaves help plants to grow and grow.

Leaves do not hunt. They do not chew.
Busy leaves make plant food.
From sunlight, air, and water,
leaves help plants make food.

Busy, busy, busy leaves
doing things we cannot see.
When busy leaves make food, it's not a trick.
It's called photosynthesis! Photosynthesis!

Come on over into the shade,
where leaves flutter, bend, and sway
on roses, grasses, and pine trees.
Broad, thin, or spiky—they're all leaves!

Leaves do not hunt. They do not chew.
Busy leaves make plant food.
From sunlight, air, and water,
leaves help plants make food.

Busy, busy, busy leaves
doing things we cannot see.
When busy leaves make food, it's not a trick.
It's called photosynthesis! Photosynthesis!

Farmers grow leaves that are good for you.
Leaves are food that you eat, too:
lettuce, spinach, and kale galore,
cabbage, collards, and so much more!

Be a tree with your leaves up high.
Reach toward the sun and sway side to side.
Plant your feet like they're tree roots.
Be a tree making yummy plant food.

Leaves do not hunt. They do not chew.
Busy leaves make plant food.
From sunlight, air, and water,
leaves help plants make food.

Busy, busy, busy leaves
doing things we cannot see.
When busy leaves make food, it's not a trick.
It's called photosynthesis! Photosynthesis!

Leaves do not hunt. They do not chew.
Busy leaves make plant food.
From sunlight, air, and water,
leaves help plants make food.

Busy, busy, busy leaves
doing things we cannot see.
When busy leaves make food,
it's not a trick.
It's called photosynthesis!
Photosynthesis!

Busy, Busy Leaves

Hip Hop (pop/world)
Drew Temperante

Intro

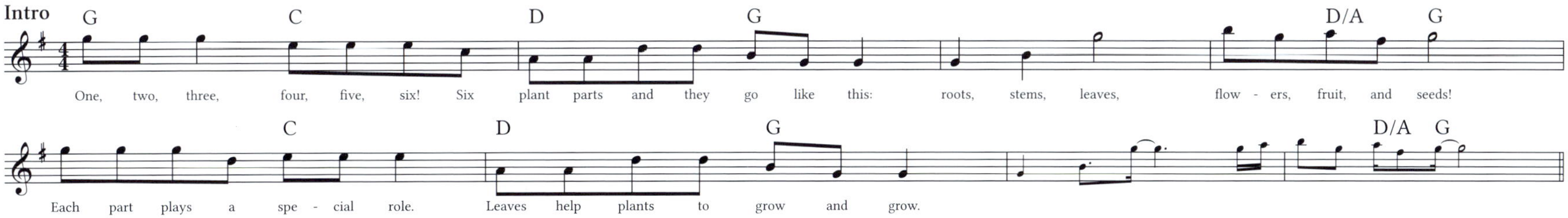

Chorus

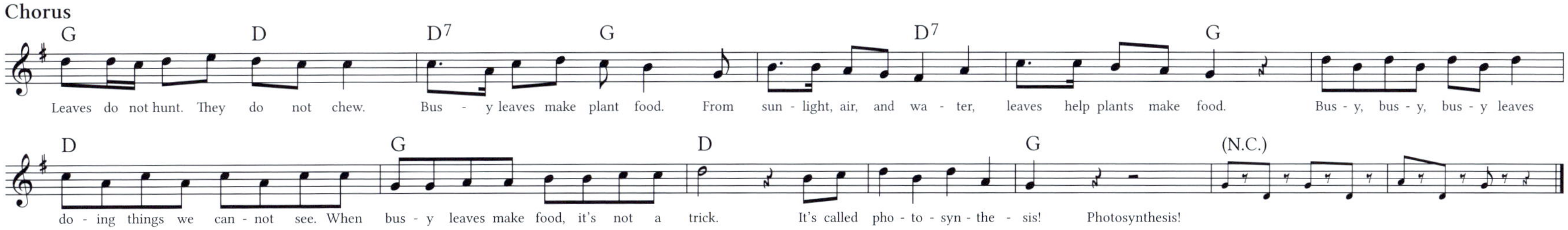

Verse

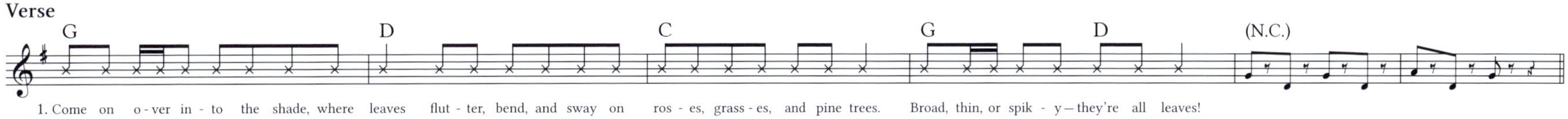

Chorus

Verse 2
Farmers grow leaves that are good for you.
Leaves are food that you eat, too:
lettuce, spinach, and kale galore,
cabbage, collards, and so much more!

Bridge

Chorus (x2)

GLOSSARY

collards—the green leaves of a vegetable related to cabbage

kale—a type of cabbage with curled leaves that do not form a dense head

photosynthesis—a process by which plants use energy from the sun to turn water and carbon dioxide into food

spiky—covered with sharp points

GUIDED READING ACTIVITIES

1. Do you have a plant in your house or classroom? Examine one of its leaves. Then try to draw that leaf.

2. Go outside with an adult and see how many different kinds of leaves you can find. What is the biggest leaf you see? What is the smallest?

3. The people on page 15 are eating a salad made of leafy vegetables. What leafy vegetables do you like to eat? Name as many as you can.

TO LEARN MORE

Bishop, Celeste. *Why Do Plants Have Leaves?* New York: PowerKids Press, 2016.

Felix, Rebecca. *What Happens to Leaves in Fall?* Ann Arbor, MI: Cherry Lake Publishing, 2013.

Glaser, Rebecca Stromstad. *Leaves*. Minneapolis: Jump!, 2013.

Throp, Claire. *All about Leaves*. Chicago: Capstone Heinemann Library, 2015.